KIDS CAN'T STOP READING THE CHOOSE YOUR OWN ADVENTURE® STORIES!

"I like Choose Your Own Adventure books because they're full of surprises. I can't wait to read more."

—Cary Romanos, age 12

"Makes you think thoroughly before making decisions."

—Hassan Stevenson, age 11

"I read five different stories in one night and that's a record for me. The different endings are fun."

—Timmy Sullivan, age 9

"It's great fun! I like the idea of making my own decisions."

—Anthony Ziccardi, age 11

And teachers like this series, too:

"We have read and reread, worn thin, loved, loaned, bought for others, and donated to school libraries our Choose Your Own Adventure books."

CHOO̶S̶ ̶ ̶ ̶ ̶ ̶ ̶ ̶ ̶ ̶ ̶ ̶ ̶ ̶RE®— AND ̶ ̶ ̶ ̶ ̶ ̶ ̶ ̶ ̶ ̶ ̶ ̶UN!

Bantam Books in the Choose Your Own Adventure® Series
Ask your bookseller for the books you have missed.

Choose Your Own Adventure Books for younger readers

THE PHANTOM SUBMARINE

BY RICHARD BRIGHTFIELD

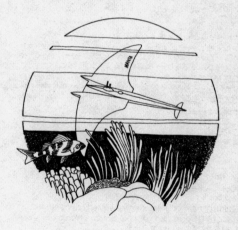

ILLUSTRATED BY RON JONES

An Edward Packard Book

BANTAM BOOKS
TORONTO · NEW YORK · LONDON · SYDNEY

RL 4, IL age 10 and up

THE PHANTOM SUBMARINE

A Bantam Book / November 1983

*CHOOSE YOUR OWN ADVENTURE® is a registered
trademark of Bantam Books, Inc. Registered in U.S. Patent and
Trademark Office and elsewhere.*

*Original Conception of Edward Packard
Front cover art by Ralph Reese*

ISBN 0-553-23635-0

Published simultaneously in the United States and Canada

---

*Bantam Books are published by Bantam Books, Inc. Its trade-
mark, consisting of the words "Bantam Books" and the por-
trayal of a rooster, is Registered in U.S. Patent and Trademark
Office and in other countries. Marca Registrada. Bantam
Books, Inc., 666 Fifth Avenue, New York, New York 10103.*

PRINTED IN THE UNITED STATES OF AMERICA

O   0 9 8 7 6 5 4 3 2 1

To Irene and Frank

THE
PHANTOM
SUBMARINE

WARNING!!!!

Do not read this book straight through from beginning to end! These pages contain many different adventures you can have as you search the seas. From time to time as you read along, you will be asked to make decisions and choices. Your choices may lead to success or disaster!

Your adventures are the result of your choices. *You* are responsible because *you* choose! After you make your choice, follow the instructions to see what happens next.

Think carefully before you make a move. One mistake could trap you under the North Pole or sweep you out into the depths of the ocean—or it *might* lead you to the phantom submarine.

Good luck!

It is late afternoon, just about the time your father is due home from work. You are sitting in the living room reading a book when the pages begin to blur. Your head begins to buzz. Strange images swirl before your eyes. Two large forms appear to collide. You can't make out exactly what they are, but they could be cars. Then the images fade, and the page is clear again.

Suddenly, there is a screech of brakes in front of your house, and then a loud BANG! You run to the window. A car has smashed into the front fender of your father's car just as he was turning into the driveway. Your father isn't hurt. Somehow you already *knew* that he wouldn't be.

Turn to page 4.

2

An image of something flying forms in your mind. A few seconds later, you hear a helicopter flying toward your house. It swoops low over the house and lands on a vacant lot nearby. There is a knock at the front door. This is followed by a lot of talking. Now your mother is coming up the stairs.

"Professor Conroy and some other men are here to see you," she says.

When you go downstairs, you find the professor seated on the sofa. He gets up to greet you. Two men are standing stiffly next to him. Something about them spells military, or perhaps FBI. One of the men steps forward.

"We're sorry to bother you," the man begins, "but we are here on an urgent matter. We work for a special government agency. Some time ago, we alerted all of the ESP researchers to be on the lookout for especially gifted subjects. There is a chance that you are the person who can help us work on a very special assignment. We would appreciate it if you could come with us for a couple of days to take a few tests."

"Is it all right if I go?" you ask your mother.

"You can go if you really want to," she replies. "But think it over carefully. I have my own feeling that there is much more to this than these men are telling us."

If you agree to take the tests, turn to page 5.

*If you decide not to take the tests,
turn to page 10.*

Several days later, you are going down one of the stairways at school when your head begins to buzz again. You see a falling image. You guess what it is. "Watch out!" you cry, but the student is already falling.

At dinner that evening, you tell your parents about your experiences.

"I've heard that one of the professors at the university is trying to make a scientific study of just this sort of thing," says your father. "I think the professor's name is Conroy. Tomorrow, I'll give him a call, and maybe you can meet him."

A few days later, you find yourself seated in Professor Conroy's office.

"We call this phenomenon ESP," the professor tells you, "which is short for *extrasensory perception*. It is a very rare ability. Some people with ESP can see into the future, while others are able to move or bend objects with their minds. You seem to know when something is about to happen."

Three weeks have passed since your talk with the professor. You are sitting in your room when you have that feeling again that something is about to happen.

Turn to page 2.

"I think I should go," you tell your mother. "At least I'll be able to find out what's been going on in my head."

A few hours later, the helicopter, with you, Professor Conroy, and the other two men aboard, lands in the center of a large, heavily guarded complex of buildings near Washington, D.C.

You are met by an attractive, neatly dressed woman with short hair.

"Let me introduce Dr. Thursen, Greta Thursen," says Professor Conroy. "Greta was a research associate of mine. Now she is working for the government. I'll leave you in her hands. I have to get back to my students. Good luck!"

Go on to the next page.

Dr. Thursen takes you to her office nearby.

"First," she says, "I would like you to try to guess the numbers on the backs of these special cards."

You close your eyes in concentration. "Let me think," you say. "That one is a five. The next one is a ten. . . ."

After you've gone through the whole pile, Dr. Thursen seems disappointed. "You scored a little better than fifty percent," she tells you, "but that falls within the normal margin for error. Your ESP abilities do not seem particularly strong. If you will wait here, I will go and discuss this with my associates."

As Dr. Thursen talks, you get the feeling again that something is about to happen. You sense that there is great danger just outside the office.

"Dr. Thursen, stop!" you exclaim. "Don't go out that door!"

Turn to page 8.

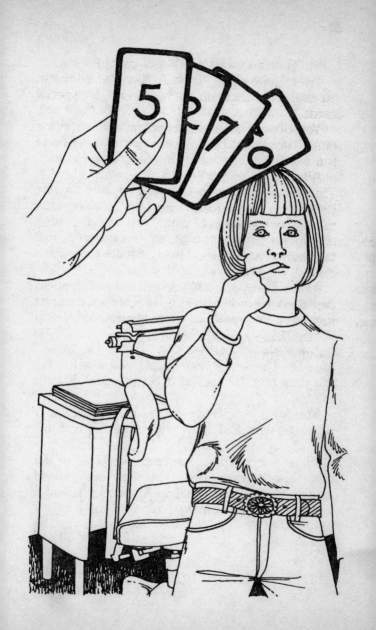

There is a loud CRASH!

"Is everyone all right in there?" someone shouts.

Dr. Thursen cautiously pulls open the door, now pushed slightly off its hinges. The back of a large truck is jammed up against the outside of the building. An ashen-faced driver appears around the side of the truck.

"My brakes failed just as I was backing up," he explains.

Dr. Thursen turns to you. "You do have some remarkable abilities, after all," she says. "You probably saved my life. I think you are exactly the person we have been looking for."

The two men who came with you on the helicopter arrive out of breath. Dr. Thursen explains to them what happened. They are now all looking at you.

"I think we've learned what we need to know," says Dr. Thursen. "How would you like to play the role of ESP specialist on a research submarine?"

You are a bit flabbergasted, to say the least. "I don't see what ESP has to do with a submarine," you say.

"This is no ordinary submarine," one of the men says. "It is designed so that ESP can be used as a special backup warning. We had planned a long land-based training program, but now we are pressed for time. You will have to learn on the job. At sea!"

Go on to the next page.

"Wait a minute," you say. "My family expects me home in a couple of days."

"I know," says the man. "We will talk to your parents and explain that what you will be doing is vital to the nation's security."

"National security!" you exclaim. "Really?"

"Ordinarily," says the man, "we wouldn't tell you about it until after you agreed to help us. But since it may influence your decision, we will. Ships at sea—all over the world—are disappearing without a trace. They're here one second, gone the next. Particularly submarines. We don't know why. The Russians are losing as many as we are. This mission is a very dangerous one, so it is your privilege to refuse."

If you agree to embark immediately on this mission, turn to page 13.

If you tell them that you need more time to think it over, turn to page 19.

Your mother may be right. There could be more to this than meets the eye.

"I don't think I want to do this right now," you say.

"But this may be vital to your country, and . . . and *you* are refusing to help us?" says one of the men, getting red in the face with anger.

"I think it is time for you gentlemen to leave," your mother says.

Go on to the next page.

The red-faced man suddenly steps forward and grabs you by the arm.

"If you don't want to come with us voluntarily, we'll just have to make you!"

Turn to page 21.

"We're getting underway," says Hornbolt. "This wide, underwater tunnel is carved out of solid rock. It leads to Puget Sound a few miles away, which empties into the Pacific. Whoever or whatever is preying on our ships seems to keep a close watch on our ports and shipyards. Many new ships have disappeared only a few miles after being launched. That is why we are being so careful this time."

"I still don't understand where I come in," you say.

"This ship has the most advanced electronic gear developed, but it is not enough," explains the captain. "The electronic sensors of the other ships apparently failed. We are depending on your ESP abilities to give us an extra warning of danger. In addition, you will be called upon to make some crucial decisions that depend on your special psychic ability. You may even have to take control of the *Manta* if our electronic systems fail."

"That's quite a lot to expect from me," you say. "I don't really know if I can do it."

"Don't worry about that," says the captain. "As soon as we reach the open sea, you'll start your training."

Turn to page 16.

The mysterious disappearance of the ships intrigues you. You agree to help.

Hours later, you are aboard a transcontinental military jet on the way to a shipyard on the West Coast. Dr. Greta Thursen and the two men are with you.

"I am Captain Hornbolt," says the man who has been doing most of the talking. "I will be in command of the submarine. Mr. Higby here is a very experienced navigator. Dr. Thursen will also be with us on the voyage. The ship itself will have a crew of one hundred and fifty, not counting the four of us."

Go on to the next page.

14

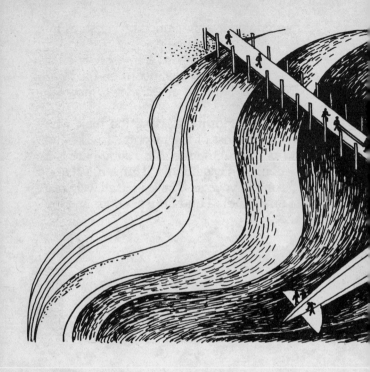

After you land, the captain shows you around.
You follow him to the entrance of a three-story
building and then into an elevator. The elevator
goes down through several underground floors
and stops.

The door opens on to a long corridor. You
follow it to another door that leads to a metal
balcony. The scene is breathtaking. You are
standing high above an enormous man-made
cavern. High-intensity lights are placed at inter-
vals along the towering walls. Far below, tiny
figures swarm over a large, rounded vessel, float-

MANTA

ing on an artificial lake in the center of the cavern floor. It doesn't seem like any ship or submarine that you have ever seen. It has a wide, curving front like a wing. Behind this is a long, tapering, taillike stern. It looks like an enormous manta ray.

"I think you can see," says the captain, "why we have named this ship the *Manta*. The workmen are completing the final tests. Unfortunately, we won't have a formal launching."

Turn to page 17.

16

Soon you are there. Greta Thursen arrives in the control room and shows you a special concentration booth. You sit inside on a comfortable reclining chair. Even though the booth is small, you are surrounded by hundreds of dials, monitor screens, and electronic switches.

"Wow! This all looks so complicated," you say. "I feel as if I'm inside a space capsule."

"Forget about all these gadgets," Dr. Thursen tells you. "This booth will be totally dark and soundproof when you are concentrating. That should help you to focus on your subconscious mind. Now, whatever is taking our ships could be anywhere in the ocean, anywhere in the world. Concentrate, and if you have any feelings as to where it might be, we'll head in that direction."

You close your eyes and try to sense the location of the mysterious force that captures ships.

If your ESP is telling you to go north toward the Arctic, turn to page 42.

If your ESP is telling you to go south toward the South Pacific, turn to page 20.

Another elevator takes you down to the operational level, where you board the ship. Captain Hornbolt proudly takes you through the crew's quarters, the kitchen, dining hall, engine room, and the torpedo room.

"Besides the torpedoes," says the captain, "we have missile launchers. Their warheads, though not nuclear, are very powerful. We also have a small undersea scout craft housed in a special compartment that can be flooded and opened up to the outside while the *Manta* is still submerged."

You end up in a large, circular, and dimly lighted control room.

Suddenly, various buzzers and signal horns begin to sound throughout the ship. The doors to the control room close with a gentle thud as the watertight compartments of the ship are secured. The floor sways slightly beneath you.

The *Manta* sinks straight down into the artificial lake for about a minute, then heads forward.

Turn to page 12.

"I don't think I can decide so quickly about something so important," you say.

Dr. Thursen arranges for the helicopter to ferry you back home.

"Try to decide soon," she says. "All our plans depend on your answer."

Back home, you find it difficult to sleep. You keep having nightmares about disappearing ships and the innocent people disappearing with them.

However, the next night you have a particularly vivid dream in which you see yourself trapped in a disabled and sunken submarine. You are rapidly running out of oxygen. Even though it is a dream, you *know* that this would be your fate if you went along.

The next morning you call Dr. Thursen.

"I really think I need more time to develop my ESP," you say lamely.

Dr. Thursen is not as disappointed as you thought she would be. Anyway, you have a feeling that someday you *will* use your psychic powers for the good of mankind. But not right now.

The End

"Something tells me *south*," you say. "But remember that this is my first try."

"Can you tell me what you felt when you decided?" Dr. Thursen asks.

"I'm not really sure," you answer. "I seemed to get a feeling of warmth, and I could see some swaying forms. Palm trees?"

"You will soon have it under control," says Dr. Thursen. "This is your first mission. You'll need time to get used to using your ESP."

Turn to page 22.

Professor Conroy and the other man quickly step in and pull him away.

"We're really sorry about this," says Professor Conroy. "We've all been under a lot of strain. Some of us are at breaking point. If you should change your mind about the tests, please contact me at the university."

Professor Conroy and the two men walk over to the helicopter and take off. You'll always wonder what they *really* wanted from you.

The End

In the following weeks, as the *Manta* silently glides beneath the water, heading south, you learn to "tune in" to your subconscious. You also familiarize yourself with numerous video screens and electronic sensors in your booth. You learn how to use the circuitry in the walls, designed to collect and amplify your brain waves. These waves are able to activate special controls that can operate the ship in an emergency. You keep watching the biofeedback screen, training your mind to produce different brain-wave patterns,

each of which is programmed to give a specific command to the ship.

It is while practicing with these controls one day that you suddenly sense a menace near the sub. Something is out there in the sea. Something dark and evil.

Go on to the next page.

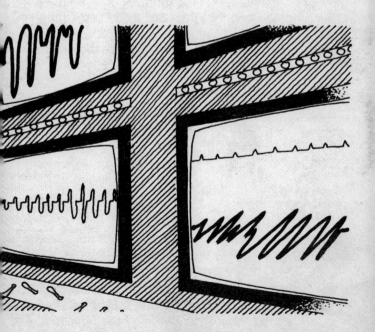

24

The conventional warning devices of the *Manta* fail to pick up anything, but your subconscious mind is filled suddenly with a feeling of dread—a dread you can't explain.

You barely have time to warn the captain when suddenly the power and control circuits in the submarine go out. The *Manta* coasts to a standstill. There is confusion throughout the ship as the crew tries in vain to restore power. You sense that the ship is surrounded by a number of small subs—you can "see" them in your mind—closing in like a pack of sharks. You know that they are about to attack. This is the moment your training has prepared you for. You have to do something fast. Luckily, the ship can be controlled by your brain waves. Immediately, you activate the emergency controls.

If you quickly take the ship to the surface, turn to page 69.

If you dive the ship at the fastest possible speed, hoping to shake off the attackers, turn to page 27.

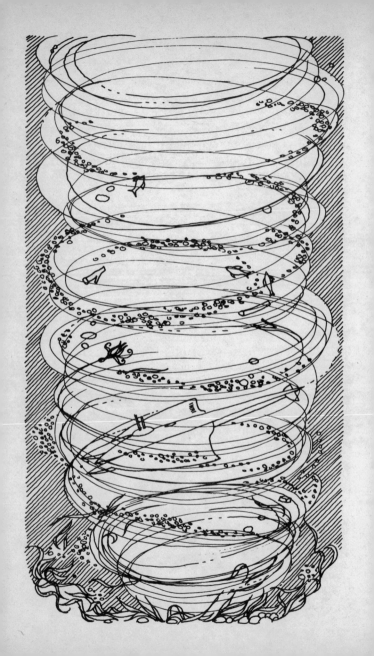

Your mind quickly forms the thought-wave pattern necessary to make the *Manta* dive at maximum speed. The ship moves fast—very fast.

"I think we did it," you say. " I don't feel the presence of the attacking subs any more."

"So that's what it was," says Hornbolt. "I'm glad we got away. But what's happening now? We seem to be spinning around."

"It feels like a giant undersea whirlpool," you say. "We're being sucked down toward the bottom at a rapid rate. And I can't stop it!"

There is a nerve-jarring crash as you hit bottom.

"All hands check for damage," orders the captain.

A few tense minutes later, Hornbolt goes through the damage reports as they are brought back to the control room.

"There doesn't seem to be much structural damage inside," he says. "Only some broken light bulbs and a few pipes twisted out of position. It's harder to tell what has been done to the outside. How about going out in the scout craft to take a look?"

If you think it is a good idea to take out the scout craft, turn to page 30.

If you think it might be better to try to raise the sub off the ocean bottom, turn to page 76.

28

"I think we should continue to search the sea bottom," you say. "A strong current could have freed the *Manta* and carried her somewhere else."

You and Hornbolt make a careful search. You keep a watchful eye on the gauges that indicate how much fuel and oxygen are left.

You see nothing in the canyon.

"I think it's time we went to the surface," you say. "My head is starting to buzz, and I don't like what it's telling me."

Halfway to the surface, your fuel and oxygen run out. Soon a lifeless scout craft is swept along with the undersea currents.

The End

The cave leads into a huge undersea amphitheater. The water is crystal clear, almost as transparent as air. The entire cavern, several miles across, glows with a soft light. The vast floor is covered with multicolored corals of every kind and description.

In the center of the cavern, still some distance off, is an immense, curious-looking rectangular structure. For a moment, you think it might be a huge solid block, then you notice small round openings near the bottom of the structure.

"Look," says Hornbolt, "our pressure gauge shows only forty feet of water pressure. Is that possible? We must be down a couple of thousand feet, at least. If this pressure reading is correct, it means that we can use our face masks and small oxygen tanks to explore that structure. Do you sense any danger here?"

If your ESP tells you that it is safe to explore the structure, turn to page 32.

If you sense that it might be too dangerous, turn to page 74.

30

"I think we should get a look at the outside of the hull before we do anything else," you say.

You and Hornbolt climb into the scout craft, a disk-shaped vessel with a large central bubble like that of a helicopter. Twin water jets push it along underwater. The little craft heads out into this strange world, its headlights probing the darkness of the sea depths.

Hornbolt turns the craft so that your beam of light illuminates the outside of the *Manta*. You see that the "tail" of the ship is dug into the ocean bottom. You circle around.

"Look at that," says Hornbolt. "Steep rock walls on every side of us! It looks as if we crashed into an undersea canyon with overhanging cliffs above us."

Turn to page 34.

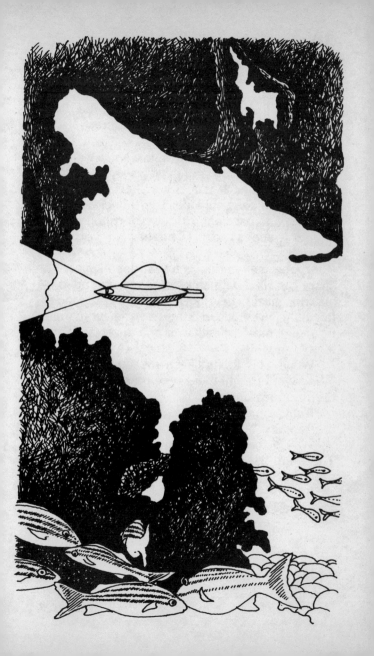

"Let's explore," you say. "I don't sense any danger."

"Then I'll show you how to put on the diving equipment stored in the scout craft," says Hornbolt.

The two of you leave through a small air lock in the back of the craft and head toward one of the round openings. It is really a short tunnel, brilliantly lit inside. You enter the tunnel and soon come to a translucent window. Hornbolt raps on it and it slides open. The two of you swim through.

Beyond the window is a vast open space. The "floor" is filled with ships of every description— ancient galleys, full-rigged sailing ships, modern freighters, even ocean liners . . . and submarines, from the most primitive to the most advanced atomic models.

"Wow! This looks like a museum," you say. "Whoever brought these here must be causing all the disappearances."

"It gives me the shivers, whatever it is," says the captain. "I think we should get out of here."

"Wait a minute," you say. "Look over there. Those are the strangest-looking vessels I've ever seen. Let's get a closer look."

"Are you absolutely sure we're still safe down here?" asks Hornbolt.

Go on to the next page.

*If you are beginning to sense danger,
turn to page 109.*

*If you are sure it's still safe,
turn to page 83.*

As you explore the sides of the canyon, you spot the opening to a large undersea cave. You hover by the entrance.

"Are my eyes playing tricks?" you ask. "Or is there a gleam of light in that cave?"

"Could be some phosphorescent sea creature," says Hornbolt, "or something else. . . . I'd like to get a look at it."

The light gets brighter the deeper you go into the cave.

"No sea creature could make that bright a light," says Hornbolt.

Turn to page 29.

A delegation from the captives of the underwater city soon comes to visit you. They are planning an escape attempt. You find out that they are always planning escape attempts.

None of them ever succeeds. At least it helps to pass the time.

The End

The light itself begins to grow and expand, and then it takes the form of a cathedrallike structure of ice. It is crescent-shaped, with the curve at the back rising high up into the sky where the tall,

luminous shafts of ice become intertwined with the swirling colors of the arctic aurora borealis.

Turn to page 106.

You have the horrible feeling that the *Manta* is about to be added to the underwater museum.

"I can fire our torpedoes," says Hornbolt, "if you think it will help."

You concentrate as hard as you can.

If your subconscious says that firing the torpedoes will help, turn to page 70.

If you sense that it is better to wait, turn to page 40.

"The odds are stacked against us," you say. "I have the feeling that they can blow us up any time they want to."

Your ship pulls up alongside the dock within the gigantic sub. You, the captain, the navigator, and Dr. Thursen step out onto the broad surface of the dock.

"Walk straight ahead," commands the voice, "and through the door you see before you."

There is a small, gleaming rectangle of greenish-yellow light at the far end of the dock. You head toward it.

On the other side of the door, you find yourselves in a wide, carpeted corridor. A continuous window of green glass, the kind you see in aquariums, lines both sides.

"That must be water on the other side of the glass," you say. "I can see dim shapes swimming back and forth. Some sort of creatures are looking at us."

"You're right," says Dr. Thursen. "I have the queasy feeling that *we* are the fish in the fishbowl this time."

Turn to page 45.

"I definitely think we should wait," you tell Hornbolt.

After a few minutes, you realize that the *Manta* has been swallowed up by something. Whatever it is, you are surrounded by it. Underwater lights from above show a vast expanse of crystal-clear water in every direction—ending in sheer, metallic walls.

"Where do you think we are?" asks Dr. Thursen.

"We're inside some huge undersea craft," you say.

"No submarine could be *this* large," says Hornbolt.

Suddenly, a loud, booming voice reverberates through the *Manta*: "Bring your ship up and prepare to dock," it orders. "The captain of your ship and his staff will disembark first. The crew will follow. All weapons must be left behind. Any disobedience will be punished harshly."

Go on to the next page.

"I'm taking the ship up," Hornbolt announces over the ship's loudspeakers.

The *Manta* breaks the surface of a broad lake, *inside* the phantom sub. Something has hold of your ship and is propelling it rapidly toward a dock.

"Are we going to give up without a fight?" asks Dr. Thursen.

If your ESP tells you to obey the orders from the voice, turn to page 39.

If your ESP tells you to fight, turn to page 86.

"I think we should head north," you say. "While I was concentrating, strange, jagged shapes appeared before my eyes. I couldn't quite get them into focus. They were definitely white. I felt a cold chill. The forms could be icebergs."

In the days that follow, you work on developing your ESP, particularly the ability to control the ship with your mind. The *Manta* keeps heading north.

"How far north do you think we should go?" Hornbolt asks you.

"I'm not completely sure," you answer, "but I'm certain we're going in the right direction."

"A few days more," says Hornbolt, "and we'll be in the Bering Strait, heading for the North Pole. I'll go as far north as I can, and then we'll turn back."

Turn to page 46.

"I still think it would be safer if we explored with the scout craft first," you say.

You and Hornbolt pilot the small craft through the tunnel blasted by the torpedoes. You're disappointed to discover that it opens into still another, larger area surrounded by ice. But there is something very strange about it. A bluish-green light illuminates this vast chamber. Also, your instruments indicate that the water is twenty degrees warmer than it should be.

"Probably some kind of volcanic activity on the bottom of the sea," says Hornbolt.

"That could be," you say, "but my special sense is telling me that it is even stranger than that."

For a second, Hornbolt looks scornful, but suddenly he sees something that makes him gape in astonishment.

Turn to page 49.

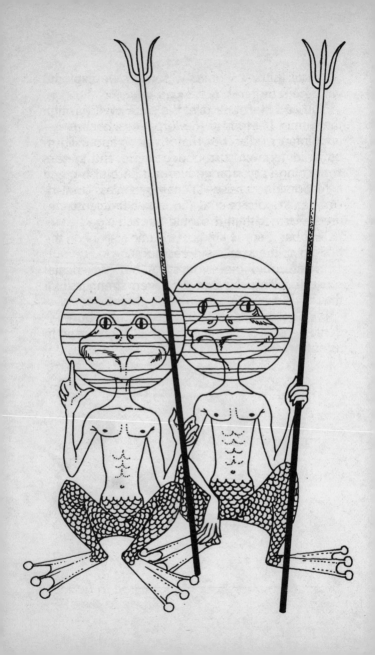

A dozen short creatures with greenish-gray skin and webbed feet and hands appear in the corridor ahead of you. Their heads are covered with transparent helmets filled with water. Each creature carries a long, three-pronged weapon. They herd the four of you down to the end of the corridor and through a revolving door.

You find yourselves in a huge, glass-domed room. In the center of the room a helmeted creature sits on a large throne. He is much bigger than the others.

"So another ship has been sent to pollute our sacred seas," he says. "We are but one of the many sea peoples who have lived peacefully in the oceans for millions of years. As your species evolved on the land above the waters, it gradually contaminated the seas. We have been patient, but now you are dumping radioactive wastes into the ocean. We must find a way to stop this, or we will be destroyed. The four of you have talents we can use. We ask you to join us for the good of your own people as well as ours. Perhaps together we can find a solution."

Dr. Thursen, the captain, and the navigator all turn and look at you. They are hoping that you will know what to do.

If you agree to join the sea people,
turn to page 80.

If you need more time to decide,
turn to page 94.

Coming out of the Bering Strait, the sub soon passes under the polar ice pack. The broad Chukchi Sea is getting shallower and shallower, and the ice above is getting thicker and thicker.

"There're sixty feet of ice above us," says Hornbolt, "and only thirty feet between the ice and the sea bottom. That gives us only a few feet to spare. I think it's time for us to get out of here before we get stuck."

"You're right," you say, even though some strong force keeps drawing you toward the North Pole.

The *Manta* turns in a wide arc and heads back toward the strait.

"Something is wrong," says Higby, the navigator. "My instruments show that the clearance between the ice and the sea bottom is getting narrower—even though we are heading back the way we came."

The command "Stop all engines!" echoes throughout the ship.

Go on to the next page.

The *Manta* drifts to a stop before a solid wall of underwater ice.

"We're trapped!" exclaims Higby. "There is nothing but solid ice around us."

"We still have a few tricks up our sleeve," says Hornbolt. "We can try to blast our way through the ice with our torpedoes, or we can drill an escape tunnel up through the ice to the surface. Both ways are dangerous. We'll have to leave it up to our expert to decide."

"I'm not sure how much help I can be with this one, but I'll do my best," you say.

If your ESP tells you to blast the ice with the torpedoes, turn to page 50

If your ESP tells you to drill a hole to the surface, turn to page 92.

"Look at that!" exclaims Hornbolt. "A full-rigged nineteenth-century sailing ship, with the sails still set! What a marvel of preservation. The sails flapping in these undersea currents make it look as if it's sailing in the wind."

Turn to page 52.

"Let's blast through the ice," you say.

"Okay, then, I'll take the *Manta* as far back from the wall of ice as I can, and then let go with a couple of torpedoes," says Hornbolt.

Even though the sub is positioned almost a mile away from the ice, the explosions rock the *Manta* as the shock waves bounce back and forth.

The torpedoes blast open a large hole.

"There seems to be clear water beyond that hole," says Higby. "The opening is just large enough for the *Manta* to squeeze through."

"Do you think we should blast it with another torpedo?" asks Dr. Thursen.

"No," answers Hornbolt. "That could just as easily close up the hole. Let's get through there fast. This may be our last chance to escape, and we may not have much time left."

"I think that we should examine the opening and what lies beyond before we risk the *Manta*," you say.

"I still think we should get through while we can," says Hornbolt.

If you insist on going out in the scout craft first, turn to page 43.

If Hornbolt has convinced you that the Manta *should try to squeeze through the hole now, turn to page 100.*

"It seems to be giving off some kind of energy. I can feel it," you say. "And there's a dim light coming out of the portholes and upper hatches. I think that we should investigate the inside of the ship."

The scout craft settles down on the deck beside the forward hatch. The light coming from belowdecks is surprisingly bright.

"What do you think is making that light?" you ask.

"There's only one way you're going to find out," says Hornbolt. "We have cold suits and other arctic scuba gear aboard. And this water is warmer than the usual arctic water."

"You don't mean you want me to go down inside the ship alone, do you?" you ask.

"I do think it might be safer if one of us kept watch at the top of the hatch," says Hornbolt. "But I'll leave it up to you."

If you think that the two of you should go down together, turn to page 98.

If you agree with Hornbolt, and decide to go down alone, turn to page 55.

You tell Hornbolt your plan to run the *Manta* into the ice wall.

"I know it sounds crazy," you say, "but I'm *sure* it will work."

"Well, we have to try *something*," says Hornbolt. "In the past few minutes, the water temperature has suddenly dropped to twenty-six degrees—colder than the freezing point of sea water."

The *Manta* heads for the wall of ice. You believe the skipper, but you brace yourself for a crash anyway. Your ship slides into the "ice" as if it were nothing more than a thick fog.

"Well, I'll be darned!" exclaims Hornbolt.

"I'm just glad it worked," you say.

"I told ye so," the skipper says to you. "Now head south for another dozen leagues, and we'll be free of this arctic prison."

The *Manta* heads back toward Alaska.

Just as you pass Nunivak Island, the ship's sonar starts picking up some strange signals. At the same time, your head starts to buzz. An alarm rings in your subconscious.

Turn to page 56.

The captain is probably right, you think. If the two of you go down together and both get into trouble, you're out of luck.

Leaving Hornbolt at the top of the hatch, you climb down, half expecting to see a crew of skeletons. But what you *do* find is even more amazing.

You make your way down a short corridor and into a large cabin, no doubt belonging to the ship's captain. There behind a small desk is the luminous figure of the captain himself. You are not sure, but you think you can see right through him.

"So ye took a hundred years to find me," says the figure. "And what news of me crew? Did they make it back?"

You stand there dumfounded for a moment.

"I . . . I'm sorry I don't have any information," you say. "We just stumbled on your ship trying to find our way out of this maze of ice."

"Ah, yes," says the figure, "this confounded ice. Sucked me ship to the bottom, it did. The crew escaped, but I waited too long. Seems as if I've been locked in this icy tomb for an eternity. But this has its good side too, matey. I know its every whim and every turn, I do."

Turn to page 57.

"I have a feeling that something bad is about to happen," you tell the skipper.

"Aye, matey, I do meself. It's them evil varmints. We would run into them again, curse the luck. Best ye stop the ship and lie as quiet as a mouse and hope they pass us by."

You express your concern to Hornbolt.

"This ship is fast. Maybe we could outrun them," says Hornbolt.

If your ESP tells you to lie low and wait, turn to page 110.

If your ESP tells you to try to outrun the danger, turn to page 58.

"Yer not the first to come here that way," says the figure. "A while back—half a year, I reckon—another underwater ship, a huge one, came. It was manned by strange creatures—evil little varmints they was."

"That sounds like what we've been looking for," you say.

"Well, if yer lookin' for the likes o' them, then Lord rest yer soul."

"No, I mean we're trying to stop them," you say. "Now, I'd appreciate it if you could tell me how to get our ship out of here."

"Not unless ye take me with ye," says the ship's captain. "I must check on me crew. They set sail for Sitka, Alaska, long ago."

"All right, then," you say. "Let's go, Captain."

"Ye can just call me Skipper, if ye like."

Together you make your way up to the top deck of the old ship.

"I want you to meet my friend, the skipper," you say to Hornbolt once inside the scout craft.

"You want me to meet—*who*?" asks Hornbolt. "I don't see anyone but you."

"The skipper is . . . You mean you can't see him?" you ask.

Turn to page 59.

58

"You're right," you say to Hornbolt. "I think we should try to get away."

He orders full speed ahead.

Everything is all right for an hour, then alarm signals go off throughout the *Manta*. The companionways are suddenly filled with a blue haze. Everything in the *Manta* glows as if it had an inner heat, but all the surfaces are cold to the touch. The walls of the sub begin to "dissolve." You can see right through them. The hull becomes transparent. You can see fish swimming in the water just outside. But the water doesn't rush in.

Dr. Thursen and Hornbolt are standing dumfounded in the middle of the control room. You and the skipper (who is still invisible to everyone but you) are standing beside them. A blue mist envelops the four of you. When it clears, you are all standing in what looks like a huge stone cavern. Hornbolt is about to say something when a ray of light hits him from above. He turns transparent and disappears, leaving a small column of blue smoke. Then Dr. Thursen disappears in the same way. Now it is your turn. You have just enough time to look at your hand and see it fading before you black out.

Turn to page 73.

The skipper whispers in your ear, "There's them that can see and hear me, and them that can't."

"Are you certain you're all right?" Hornbolt asks you.

"Oh, sure," you say. "I was just kidding there for a moment."

You, Hornbolt, and, of course, the skipper head back to the *Manta*. Dr. Thursen and Higby have a lot of questions. You manage to evade answering.

"I need a few minutes alone," you say.

Alone with the skipper, you ask him what to do now.

"All right, matey, just head full sail due east, and then we'll tack to the south."

"But there's a solid wall of ice in that direction," you protest.

"Ye just think there's a wall there."

"I can't really believe that. All our instruments show that it's solid."

"I don't ken yer fancy instruments, matey. All I know is what I know."

"I'll have to concentrate hard on that before I do anything," you say.

If your ESP tells you to go along with the skipper and advise Hornbolt to head for the ice wall, turn to page 53.

If your ESP tells you not to head for the wall, turn to page 101.

60

"I don't know if I can make it," you tell the skipper, "but I'll give it one more try."

You struggle up the last hill. Before you reach the top, you are crawling on your hands and knees, your hands torn and bloody from the rocks.

There it is. The *Manta* is anchored nearby in an ice-free cove. You have no trouble making it to the ship. The sight of the *Manta* makes you forget how tired you are.

Turn to page 84.

"I guess I'll go to Erbolt," you say. "Anything sounds better than working in a mine under the North Pole."

"That is a wise choice," says Boron. "Now, if you will just step over here, I'll adjust the controls."

"It's wiser for ye than that varmint thinks," says the skipper's voice. "I think I've got their devilish contraption figured out. Made some adjustments of me own. When ye step into their beam of light, just keep yer eyes tightly closed."

Boron gives you a push toward the beam. You stumble into it. As you do, he starts punching a combination of buttons on a control panel.

Suddenly there is a terrific flash of light that shines brightly through your closed eyelids.

Turn to page 66.

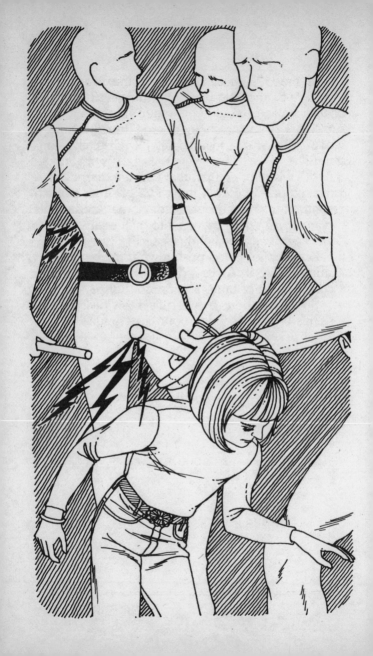

You brace yourself, expecting the *Manta* to topple over the edge of this strange pit in the ocean. Instead, there is a sudden crash as if the sub had been rammed by a large, invisible ship. You are thrown to the deck. You look up and see hundreds of tall, humanoid creatures appearing out of nowhere and swarming onto the deck. Each creature holds a short rod that sends out a paralyzing beam. The crew is overwhelmed.

You try to grab an attacker, but one of the beams hits you. You are frozen in an awkward bent-over position with your arms grabbing at the air. Suddenly, you know how a statue would feel, if it could feel.

Turn to page 75.

64

"My name is Boron," says the creature in the center of the room. "I am from the planet Erbolt. I am in charge of the Erboltian outpost here on your miserable planet. We have many uses for you Earthlings. We find it amusing to give you a choice of your fate. We can send you to Erbolt, where we use Earthlings as—what can I call it?— as 'pets,' you might say. Barring static in transmission, you should arrive in good-enough shape. On the other hand, you can remain on this planet and work in our titanium mines under the North Pole."

*If you choose to be a "pet" on Erbolt,
turn to page 61.*

*If you would rather stay on Earth, even if you
have to work in the mines, turn to page 102.*

You can't go on. You don't realize that your fatigue is one of the symptoms of freezing to death. The ghost of the skipper has moved on ahead. When he returns, you are too far gone.

"Well, matey, I think ye and me will be good company for a very long time," says the skipper.

You have become another ghost of the Arctic.

The End

The bright light dims a bit, and you open your eyes just enough to see what's going on. The Erboltians are now running blindly around the room and colliding with each other. Whenever they collide, they vanish in a puff of blue smoke.

"Heavens o' fire!" shouts the skipper. "I made their fiendish contraption blow up in their evil little faces, I did. And while they're thrashin' around and disappearin', we'll escape through this tunnel I've discovered."

You run down a long passageway carved out of rock. Out of breath, you finally reach the exit. You emerge high up on the side of a rocky hill. Far below is the ocean, covered with ice floes as far as you can see.

"From their chatter," says the skipper, "I gathered that yer ship be around here somewhere—in one of them coves down there, I reckon. Maybe if we troop over to that ridge, we can see it."

Turn to page 68.

An icy wind is blowing up from the sea. The skipper in his turtleneck sweater doesn't seem to feel the cold, but you sure do. After climbing over a few more ridges in your search for the *Manta*, you feel frozen stiff. You no longer have any sensation in your arms or legs, and you are tired, so tired.

"I can't go any farther," you say. "I've had it."

"Just one more ridge, matey. You can make it."

"One more, one more. It's always one more. I have to stop to rest, and then I'll go on," you say.

"I think we better keep goin'," warns the skipper.

If you stop to rest and tell the skipper to go on ahead, turn to page 65.

If you make a last effort to go over one more ridge, turn to page 60.

You activate the controls that turn the *Manta* sharply upward. The bow breaks the surface of the ocean.

You, Dr. Thursen, and Hornbolt follow an emergency detail out of the forward hatch and onto the deck. There are no other ships around. The empty sea stretches in all directions.

Then Dr. Thursen points behind the ship, a look of alarm on her face. "What *is* that over there?" she asks.

At first, you don't see what she is pointing to; then you see it. "It looks like an enormous depression in the ocean," you say, "and it seems to be heading in our direction."

"It could be a whirlpool of some sort," says Hornbolt.

"If it is," you say, "it's the first rectangular whirlpool I've ever heard of."

"Whatever it is," says Dr. Thursen, "we'll know in a few seconds. It's coming right at us!"

Turn to page 63.

"Fire!"

Your mind's eye follows the torpedoes racing out toward the phantom sub. Then suddenly you foresee your own doom. You know that you are powerless to escape. You can only stand in a state of shock as the torpedoes turn and come back straight at the *Manta*.

Desperately, you try to turn them aside with the power of your thought waves. You can't do it. But of course you already know the end. There is a tremendous explosion as the first one hits. Then another.

The *Manta* splits in two, and you are swept out into the depths of the ocean.

The End

"Welcome? Some welcome!" exclaims Hornbolt. "So this is how you have been seizing our ships. Sooner or later, you will be tracked down and destroyed."

"It seems more likely that you who inhabit the land will destroy yourselves first. What *we* are afraid of is that you will destroy *us* in the process."

"I don't think you are helping matters," says Dr. Thursen, "by stealing our ships and kidnapping our people."

"All those who have been seized are safe and will be released soon," says the voice. "In the meantime, we need to study your people at close range. We must find the source of your self-destructive nature. We also seek to find those among you who will work with us to help stop this senseless destruction of our shared world."

"Trying to find traitors to humanity, you mean!" shouts Hornbolt.

"They don't seem that dangerous," you whisper to Dr. Thursen. "Maybe we should give them a chance to tell us how we can help."

If you feel that you should give these creatures a chance to explain how you can help, turn to page 96.

If you agree with Hornbolt that helping them would betray mankind, turn to page 108.

When you come to, you are not transparent anymore, but you are in a strange place. You are in the center of a circle of low, desklike boxes. Behind every box is a small, squat creature. Eyes glare at you from the ends of long stalks sticking out from the top of each head. They look more like overgrown lobsters than anything else. You don't know what has happened to Dr. Thursen and Hornbolt, but the skipper is standing beside you.

"Can they see you?" you ask the skipper under your breath.

"These slimy critters can't see or hear me, thank the Lord. And I think I've figured out how they do their mischief. Keep 'em talkin', and I'll see what mischief *I* can do."

"So, Earthling," says one of the creatures, "you were searching for us, and now you've found us. Or, it seems, we've found *you*."

This is followed by a high-pitched cackling sound from all of the creatures, which you take to be laughter. Meanwhile, the skipper has disappeared.

Turn to page 64.

"This place *looks* safe enough, but something is wrong. My ESP is warning me about something—I'm not sure what," you say.

"Well, this cavern isn't going to go away," says Hornbolt. "I think the crew of the *Manta* should know what we are doing."

You turn the scout craft around and head back toward the ship.

But the *Manta* is not there. Your searchlight plays over the walls of the canyon and along the ocean bottom. You find the scar on the ocean floor where the stern of the sub had plowed into it. But there is no trace of the *Manta* itself.

"I'm not sure we should waste the last of our fuel and oxygen searching for the *Manta*," Hornbolt says. "It might be better to get up to the surface while we can. On the other hand, the ship might not have gone very far."

If your ESP tells you to keep searching the canyon for the Manta, *turn to page 28.*

If your ESP tells you to get to the surface as fast as possible, turn to page 78.

You can't move or speak, but you are still breathing and you can move your eyes. Several of the creatures pick you up and carry you toward the pit. They walk over the pit in midair, as if walking on an invisible surface. Then they make a sharp left turn, and you are inside a companionway that you can *see*. So that's it! You are in a ship that is invisible from the outside, but visible on the inside.

The creatures carry you down a long corridor and deposit you in a small circular chamber. Dr. Thursen and Hornbolt are already there, also frozen into their last movements. Slowly, sensation starts coming back to your bodies. You start to rub your arms and legs to get the circulation back.

Then a voice booms from somewhere: "Welcome aboard the vessel of the sea people."

Turn to page 71.

"I think we should try to lift the *Manta* up from the sea bottom first," you tell Hornbolt.

One end of the sub is stuck deep in the ocean floor. The *Manta* doesn't seem to budge, even though Hornbolt has all the ship's engines going at full power.

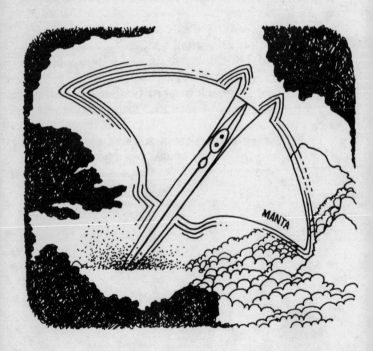

Go on to the next page.

Suddenly the sub pulls free and shoots diagonally upward.

Your ESP warns you, but it is too late.

"Stop!" you shout helplessly. "Reverse engines or something!"

The *Manta* crashes with full force into the overhanging cliff of an undersea canyon and splits apart. As the water rushes in, you try to hold your breath as long as you can—about two minutes.

The End

"Something tells me that we should get right to the surface," you say.

Hornbolt agrees. "The *Manta* could have freed herself and Higby might have taken her up," he says.

When you get to the surface, a bright red ball of sun is rising in the east.

"Down in the sea," you say, "I'd lost track of day and night."

You try to contact the *Manta* by radio. No luck.

"Look over there on the horizon," says Hornbolt. "I think that's an island."

"It looks like one to me, too," you say, "but my head is ringing with danger signals."

"We may have to land on the island to survive," says Hornbolt. "Or we could drift away from it and take our chances on being picked up by a passing ship. What should we do?"

If you decide to stay away from the island,
turn to page 87.

If you decide to explore the island,
turn to page 82.

"If what they say is true," you say, "I don't see how we can refuse to help."

"Okay, we'll give it a try," says Hornbolt, "but if they try any funny stuff, they'll suffer the consequences."

"Step into the chamber in back of the room," says the sea creature, "and we will begin."

As soon as you enter the chamber, an anesthetic gas knocks you all unconscious. When you awake, you find that you and your friends have been given a "gill" operation. Gills have been implanted to enable you to breathe underwater. You also find that tight, seamless, metal collars have been fastened around your necks. Your ESP doesn't seem to be working.

"You are now part of our organization," explains the sea creature. "The collars you are wearing contain explosive charges that can be set off, if necessary, by remote control."

"What kind of double cross is this?" shouts Hornbolt. "You didn't tell us about collars—they're symbols of slavery!"

Go on to the next page.

"Not at all," says the sea creature. "They are symbols of freedom. Now we can trust you completely, and you can go anywhere in our underwater realm. We no longer have to worry about your loyalty. *Or your obedience.*"

Eventually, you will find a way to remove the collar and return to land, but that is a long way in the future.

The End

You are very wary of this island, but you realize that you have to take a chance.

"I think we have almost enough fuel to reach the shore," says Hornbolt. "We can swim the rest of the way."

You head for the island.

Suddenly, a large, dark shape looms up in front of you. As it comes closer, you realize that it is a large warship, perhaps a missile frigate or a cruiser.

Someone is speaking through a bull horn, addressing you from the high bridge of the vessel.

"Identify yourselves," the voice commands.

Turn to page 85.

You feel it is safe enough to swim over to one of the strange ships.

"What do you make of it?" you ask Hornbolt.

"This doesn't look like an Earth-made craft at all," he says. "It's more like a spaceship from another planet."

"Let's try to get inside and see what it looks like," you say. "That door might lead into an air lock of some sort."

You and Hornbolt enter the alien craft. After passing through an air lock, you discover that you can breathe without your diving equipment. You have no trouble finding the control room. Hornbolt looks over the rows of dials and switches. You sense trouble.

"I wonder if I could operate this ship," says Hornbolt, pressing one of the many buttons on the control board.

"Stop!" you cry out. But it's too late.

Turn to page 88.

The whole crew is there, including Hornbolt and Dr. Thursen. You wonder if they went through what you did, but they can't remember anything about the previous few hours. They are certainly glad to see you.

You tell Hornbolt and Dr. Thursen about the Erboltians but not about the skipper. So they are somewhat mystified when you insist on stopping at the Alaskan city of Sitka on your way back to base.

"Maybe I ain't the only ghost still wanderin' around from them days," the skipper had said. "Maybe in Sitka . . ."

"I don't really understand why we are stopping here," says Hornbolt, "but I guess it's the least that we can do for you after all your help."

The End

"Captain Hornbolt of the United States Navy," Hornbolt shouts back. "And who are you, if I may ask?"

"Hornbolt! Stay where you are. We'll send a boat right over."

Soon a launch is heading toward you. As you board, Hornbolt suddenly exclaims, "Admiral McQuade, what are you doing here?"

"It's good to see you, Hornbolt, but my question is, what are *you* doing here?" asks McQuade. "You almost blew our timetable for raiding this island."

Turn to page 89.

"I think that if we fight back, it may help in the long run," you say.

"I agree," says Hornbolt. "We shouldn't give up without a fight—even if we lose."

Hornbolt gives the order to fire all weapons at once.

Seconds later, the inside wall of the phantom submarine reverberates with explosions from the *Manta's* missiles. The *Manta's* torpedoes rip into the landing dock and blow it to pieces.

The phantom sub strikes back with laser cannons that disintegrate the *Manta*.

At least you go down fighting. It will take years for the phantom submarine to recover from the damage the *Manta* has inflicted. By that time, others will have taken up the chase.

The End

"The bad feelings that I'm getting from that island are just too strong," you tell Hornbolt. "I think we should stay away."

In any event, a strong current is already carrying you rapidly away from the island. There is not enough power left in the craft's storage battery to operate the radio. You drift for days. The emergency rations are soon used up. Water is not so much of a problem as Hornbolt sets up a system in which water condenses on the inside of the bubble canopy of the scout craft.

You begin to lose hope.

Turn to page 91.

You hear a whirring sound as the ship begins to move straight up. You and Hornbolt are thrown back into two oversized chairs in front of the control board. A large hatch in the roof of the undersea structure opens and the spaceship zips through.

Soon it has risen out of the ocean altogether, heading upward at an ever-increasing speed. Hornbolt *would* have the bad luck to press the one button programmed to make the spaceship from Alpha Centauri return to its home planet. You are in for a long, long ride.

The End

"Raiding the island? What is this all about?" asks Hornbolt.

"This island is the headquarters of a band of modern-day pirates," explains the admiral. "They are holding many prisoners for ransom. But all of them will be free by tonight, I promise."

"Have you heard anything about my ship, the *Manta*?" asks Hornbolt. "We seem to have lost track of her."

"One of our ships has her in tow," says the admiral. "Seems she bobbed to the surface, disabled, a few hours ago. I suspect that they are quite worried about you two. I'll radio our ship at once."

You watch the raid from the bridge of the admiral's command ship. The next day, you are transferred, along with the freed prisoners, to a destroyer heading back to Seattle. For the moment, you've had enough adventure.

The End

Then you sight another island. You and Hornbolt have just enough energy left to beach the scout craft and crawl up to the line of coconut palms along the shore.

A few days of eating the wild tropical fruits on the island and you are both your old selves again. You discover a tribe of friendly Polynesians on the other side of the island. You and Hornbolt settle down for a long wait. You really enjoy it. When a ship finally does visit the island, you both decide to stay.

The End

"It seems too dangerous to start blasting down here with torpedoes," you say. "I can tell you *that* without using ESP."

"All right, then," says Hornbolt. "Let's drill a tunnel to the surface and set up our ground-to-satellite emergency communication."

There is just enough room on the deck of the *Manta* below the ice to set up the underwater laser cannon. You and Hornbolt put on arctic wet suits and diving gear and go out. The cannon is very effective. In less than an hour, it has carved out a neat, vertical tunnel.

You and Hornbolt, using special cleats on your underwater boots, push your way to the surface like rock climbers scaling a mountain. You pull up the radio equipment after you.

On the surface, you find yourselves in the midst of the long arctic night that lasts several months. The stars blaze overhead.

You are setting up your equipment when, to your astonishment, you notice a bright light in the darkness not far away.

Go on to the next page.

"Do you think there could be another ship out here in this wilderness?" you ask.

"Might be an expedition that we don't know about," says Hornbolt, "or it could be our eyes playing tricks. I think we'd better just ignore it and set up our equipment."

"It might be important," you say.

"All right, I'll let you decide what we should do," says Hornbolt.

*If you decide to explore the light,
turn to page 103.*

*If you decide to ignore it,
turn to page 97.*

"I think we need more time to think this over,"
you tell Dr. Thursen, Captain Hornbolt, and the
navigator, Mr. Higby.

The sea people give you twenty-four hours.
When you talk with their leaders again, you have
a proposal. You promise to work for the reduction
of wastes—particularly atomic wastes—being
dumped in the ocean if they will let you all go.

"Fair enough," say the sea creatures. "We will
hold you to your word. And now we wish you
good luck and farewell—for the moment."

The next thing you know, the four of you are
back on the *Manta,* heading home. You can't
remember anything that happened on the phantom submarine. You don't know why, but you
and the entire crew of the *Manta* have a burning
desire to end the pollution of the oceans. A strong
post-hypnotic suggestion has been planted
deeply and permanently in your minds.

The End

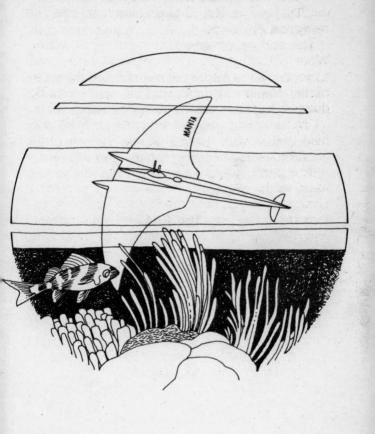

"Just how can we help?" you ask the voice.

"The four of you, if you agree, could be our eyes and ears on land. We can train you to communicate with us secretly."

As far as the rest of the crew knows, the cruise of the *Manta* was uneventful. All memory of the capture has been erased from their minds. In the years to come, you will learn much from your cooperation with the sea people. As one of the world's leading oceanographers, you will amaze the scientific world with your extensive knowledge of the oceans.

The End

"This radio link is more important than the light," you tell Hornbolt.

You work feverishly, and soon all of the equipment is set up. You notice that the light has now moved farther off. Finally, it vanishes altogether.

"I wonder what that was," you say.

"I guess we'll never know," says Hornbolt, sounding a bit regretful now that he didn't investigate.

Turn to page 107.

"Your theory about standing guard is great," you say. "The only trouble with it is that I'm *not* going down there alone."

"If that's the way you feel about it, I guess we can go down together," says Hornbolt.

Down below, you find the captain's cabin, and there on his desk is the logbook.

"This book is amazingly well preserved," says Hornbolt. "Look, I can still turn the pages, and even read the writing—though it is a bit hard to make out. Here is the last entry: 'January tenth, 1823. The invisible beast is still aboard the ship. It has murdered most of the crew. There are only a few of us left. We only know of the beast's presence by the terrible groaning of the ship's planks under the beast's fearful weight. We can hear it coming to kill us now.' "

"What is that heavy sound on the deck above?" you ask in sudden fright.

"It can't be," says Hornbolt. "I was just reading . . . and, anyway, everything is weightless underwater."

"But what if it is *so* heavy that—"

You never get to finish the sentence.

The End

"I have a feeling that we're making a mistake, but if we move quickly, we just might be able to squeeze through the hole," you say. "It might be best to try now while we have a chance."

Hornbolt shouts out commands to the crew, and the *Manta* races forward into the narrow opening. It almost makes it—but not quite.

You are halfway through the hole when the *Manta* gets stuck tight. Hornbolt does everything he can think of to get the ship loose. He reverses the engines with full power, then moves forward again. But it is no use. The ice holds you in a steellike grip. It soon begins to press down on the ship.

There is a horrible grinding sound as the ice begins to crush the *Manta* to pieces. There is no escape.

The End

Something tells you that it might not be a good idea to trust the skipper. To head into a wall of ice seems crazy.

"I think we should try our plan of tunneling to the surface," you tell Hornbolt.

But you never get the chance. The *Manta* is suddenly frozen into a solid block of ice by a stream of supercooled water. Soon everything aboard is frozen.

It will remain that way for 500 years, when you will be discovered by an archaeologist of the future. You will be restored to the living as a citizen of the twenty-fifth century.

The End

You find out that working in the mines is no fun. You have to work in the dimly lit caverns carved out by the Erboltians miles below the surface of the North Pole, where the temperature is always very, very hot.

But at least you are still on the planet Earth. And as long as you are here, there is hope of rescue.

You *will* be rescued, but not until your seventieth birthday.

The End

"I definitely think we should find out what that light is," you say.

"Okay, then, after you," says Hornbolt.

You and Hornbolt trudge through the snow toward the light. As you get closer, the wind begins to sound like a huge organ. It's uncanny. You could swear it was playing Bach.

Turn to page 36.

Suddenly, a strong beam of light stabs out of the darkness and catches the length of the *Manta*. A huge submarine looms before you. Its size almost overpowers your mind. It seems to be a

hundred times bigger than your ship. And you are being irrevocably drawn toward it.

Turn to page 38.

A long staircase appears at the front of the ice cathedral, and you and Hornbolt go up the stairs with growing amazement. The two of you stop and gape as a luminous figure, that of a woman in long robes that glow with the changing colors of the aurora above, appears in the center of this glowing palace.

"When you return to your ship, all will be well," she tells you in a musical voice.

Then the figure vanishes and the ice cathedral fades before your eyes. You wonder if it was all an illusion.

You retrace your steps in the snow by flashlight and call down to the *Manta* on the field telephone. Higby reports that the ice walls have suddenly vanished and that there is clear water to the south.

You and Hornbolt quickly return to the ship and get underway. You will have many adventures in the weeks and months ahead, but that vision in the Arctic will always haunt you.

The End

The ground-to-satellite link works perfectly, and within hours, a large transport plane is flying toward you. You have lights set up around a smooth section of ice, and the plane makes a perfect landing. You help the rest of the crew get to the surface, and then you all take off.

It was hard for you and Hornbolt to abandon the *Manta,* but the two of you are already planning a new ship and another expedition—someday.

The End

"What you are saying *sounds* good, but I don't trust you," you tell the sea people.

"I am afraid, then," says the voice, "to keep our existence secret, we will have to add you to the other captives."

The three of you are transferred to an underwater city built beneath a huge dome at the bottom of the sea. All the crews of the captured ships have been sent here to live. You are assigned quarters in one of the lower levels of the city.

Turn to page 35.

In the back of your mind, there is a foreboding of danger.

"I think that we should go back to the ship," you say.

You and the captain swim back to the scout craft and return to the *Manta*. Dr. Thursen and the crew are waiting. The engines are activated. The ship pulls free and begins to rise along the canyon walls. Soon you pass the level of the normal sea bottom.

Turn to page 104.

The skipper's advice to wait quietly on the sea bottom feels right to you. All the ship's systems are turned off. There is complete silence. No one even whispers.

The electronic screen shows a dance of waves and patterns that plots the course of something immense passing directly over you. The feeling of dread is so intense as it goes by that you grab your head to try to stop the pain.

Go on to the next page.

But slowly the feeling passes and a sense of well-being returns to you. You wonder what was above you.

You will never know how lucky you were.

The End

ABOUT THE AUTHOR

RICHARD BRIGHTFIELD is a graduate of Johns Hopkins University, where he studied biology, psychology, and archaeology. For many years he worked as a graphic designer at Columbia University. He has written *Secret of the Pyramids* in the Choose Your Own Adventure series and has coauthored more than a dozen game books with his wife, Glory. The Brightfields and their daughter, Savitri, live in Gardiner, New York.

ABOUT THE ILLUSTRATOR

RON JONES was born in Tucson, Arizona, and raised in Phoenix. A graduate of the Art Center College in Pasadena, California, he has been a magazine and book illustrator for twenty-four years. He has also worked for several major advertising agencies. Mr. Jones and his wife live in Sherman, Connecticut.

CHOOSE YOUR OWN ADVENTURE ®

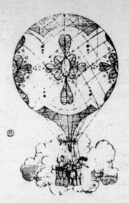

You'll want all the books in the exciting *Choose Your Own Adventure®* series offering you hundreds of fantasy adventures without ever leaving your chair. Each book takes you through an adventure—under the sea, in a space colony, on a volcanic island—in which you become the main character. What happens next in the story depends on the choices *you* make and *only you* can decide how the story ends!

Now you can have your favorite Choose Your Own Adventure® Series in a variety of sizes. Along with the popular pocket size, Bantam has introduced the Choose Your Own Adventure® series in a Skylark edition and also in Hardcover.

Now not only do you get to decide on how you want your adventures to end, you also get to decide on what size you'd like to collect them in.

SKYLARK EDITIONS

☐	15120	The Circus #1 E. Packard	$1.75
☐	15207	The Haunted House #2 R. A. Montgomery	$1.95
☐	15208	Sunken Treasure #3 E. Packard	$1.95
☐	15149	Your Very Own Robot #4 R. A. Montgomery	$1.75
☐	15308	Gorga, The Space Monster #5 E. Packard	$1.95
☐	15309	The Green Slime #6 S. Saunders	$1.95
☐	15195	Help! You're Shrinking #7 E. Packard	$1.95
☐	15201	Indian Trail #8 R. A. Montgomery	$1.95
☐	15191	The Genie In the Bottle #10 J. Razzi	$1.95
☐	15222	The Big Foot Mystery #11 L. Sonberg	$1.95
☐	15223	The Creature From Miller's Pond #12 S. Saunders	$1.95
☐	15226	Jungle Safari #13 E. Packard	$1.95
☐	15227	The Search for Champ #14 S. Gilligan	$1.95

HARDCOVER EDITIONS

☐	05018	Sunken Treasure E. Packard	$6.95
☐	05019	Your Very Own Robot R. A. Montgomery	$6.95
☐	05031	Gorga, The Space Monster #5 E. Packard	$7.95
☐	05032	Green Slime #6 S. Saunders	$7.95

Prices and availability subject to change without notice.

Buy them at your local bookstore or use this handy coupon for ordering:

WHEN YOU THINK ZINDEL, THINK BANTAM!

If you like novels whose characters are teenagers caught in the tangle of life and love—PAUL ZINDEL is right on your wavelength. All of Zindel's Young Adult novels are now available exclusively from Bantam.

☐	22540	THE GIRL WHO WANTED A BOY	$2.25
☐	22694	A STAR FOR THE LATECOMER	$2.25
☐	20172	THE UNDERTAKER'S GONE BANANAS	$2.25
☐	23975	PARDON ME, YOU'RE STEPPING ON MY EYEBALL!	$2.50
☐	20759	MY DARLING, MY HAMBURGER	$2.25
☐	20170	CONFESSIONS OF A TEENAGE BABOON	$2.25
☐	23540	THE PIGMAN	$2.50
☐	23688	PIGMAN'S LEGACY	$2.25
☐	23150	I NEVER LOVED YOUR MIND	$2.25
☐	20971	THE EFFECT OF GAMMA RAYS ON MAN-IN-THE-MOON MARIGOLDS	$2.50

Prices and availability subject to change without notice.

Buy them at your local bookstore or use this handy coupon for ordering:

Bantam Books, Inc., Dept. ZI 414 E. Golf Rd., Des Plaines, Ill 60016

Please send me the books I have checked above. I am enclosing $_____ (please add $1.25 to cover postage and handling). Send check or money order —no cash or C.O.D.'s please.

Mr/Mrs/Miss _____

Address _____

City _____ State/Zip _____

ZI—10/83

Please allow four to six weeks for delivery. This offer expires 4/84.